Can such creatures as Bigfoot and the Loch Ness monster really exist?

We know a lot about the world. You might think that there can't possibly be any mysterious or unknown large animals anymore. But don't be too sure. Large animals have remained mysterious for a long time. Only legends and rumors hinted that they existed at all. Often people who reported seeing such creatures were regarded as liars or fools. Responsible people didn't believe in monster stories. And yet the monster stories sometimes turned out to be true. The "crazy" and "foolish" people were right, and the responsible people were wrong. . . .

Critics' Corner:

"Writing in his usual brisk and lucid style leavened with the proper amount of humor, suspense, and objective questioning, the author captures readers on the first page with his statement that some of mythical monsters treated *'might be* real . . . and could be swimming or walking around right now.' "

—*School Library Journal*

". . . a competent discussion of the Loch Ness monster, the Yeti, and Bigfoot, plus various sea monsters and dragons. Arguments for and against the creatures' existence are aired, and their histories told."

—*A.L.A. Booklist*

About the Author:

DANIEL COHEN is the author of many science books for both young and old, and he is a former managing editor of *Science Digest* magazine. He has always maintained an interest in the occult, as is shown by his previous works: *In Search of Ghosts, Masters of the Occult, Mysterious Places, A Modern Look at Monsters, Myths of the Space Age, The Mysteries of Reincarnation,* and *The Magic Art of Foreseeing the Future,* which is available in an Archway Paperback edition. Mr. Cohen was born in Chicago, and he has a degree in journalism from the University of Illinois. He lives with his wife, young daughter, three dogs, and two cats in Port Jervis, New York.

THE GREATEST MONSTERS IN THE WORLD

Daniel Cohen

Illustrated with photographs and drawings

AN ARCHWAY PAPERBACK
POCKET BOOKS · NEW YORK

THE GREATEST MONSTERS IN THE WORLD

Dodd, Mead edition published 1975

Archway Paperback edition published February, 1977

The illustrations on these pages are used by permission and through the courtesy of: Rene Dahinden, pages 57, 67; Robert E. Gimlin, page 61; New York Public Library Collection, page 9; San Diego Zoo Photo by Ron Garrison, page 13; *Science Digest*, page 22; United Press International, pages 21, 46, 64; *World Book Encyclopedia*, pages 38, 41.

Published by
POCKET BOOKS, a Simon & Schuster Division of
GULF & WESTERN CORPORATION
1230 Avenue of the Americas, New York, N.Y. 10020.

Archway Paperback editions are distributed in the U.S. by Simon & Schuster, Inc., 1230 Avenue of the Americas, New York, N.Y. 10020, and in Canada by Simon & Schuster of Canada, Ltd., Markham, Ontario, Canada.

2387

In memory of **Willy Ley,**
who first introduced me
to sea monsters and dragons

CONTENTS

:- mary JANE

THE GREATEST
MONSTERS
IN THE WORLD

Monster from an Irish fairy tale

1

MONSTERS DISCOVERED

When you hear the word "monster," what do you think of?

Frankenstein? Count Dracula? The Wolf Man? Godzilla?

These are monsters, of course. But they are monsters from books and movies. At one time, people believed in such things as werewolves and vampires. Stories or movies about them can still scare us. But very few people really expect to meet a werewolf or a vampire in the flesh.

A lot of people do expect to meet Bigfoot, however. In fact, a lot of people say they already have met this monster creature. Some even say they have taken pictures of it. Bigfoot is a big, hairy, ape-like creature that is supposed to live in the forests of the United States and Canada.

A lot of people also expect to meet the Yeti or Abominable Snowman. The Yeti is a big, hairy, ape-like creature that is supposed to live in the mountains of Asia.

Thousands of people have reported seeing a huge, long-necked creature in the lake called Loch Ness in Scotland. Thousands more have reported seeing giant unknown sea monsters. Even the dragon may not be a creature out of fairy tales alone.

Bigfoot, the Yeti, the Loch Ness monster, the sea monster, the dragon—these are all "real" monsters. To be more exact, they are monsters that *might* be real. Some of these creatures could be swimming or walking around right now. We do not know for sure. There is a mystery that surrounds each one of them. These are the monsters that we are going to talk about in this book.

Can such creatures as Bigfoot and the Loch Ness monster really exist? We know a lot about the world. You might think that there can't possibly be any mysterious or unknown large animals any more. But don't be too sure. Large animals have remained mysterious for a long time. Only legends and rumors hinted that they existed at all. Often people who reported seeing such creatures were regarded as liars or fools. Responsible people didn't believe in monster stories. And yet the monster stories sometimes turned out to be true. The "crazy" and "foolish" people were right and the responsible people were wrong.

Have you ever heard of the kraken? Probably not. Two hundred years ago you would have heard of it. According to a book published at that time, the kraken was "incontestably the largest Sea-monster in the world . . ."

The book said that the kraken was "round, flat, and full of arms." Another book described a sea monster as looking like "a Tree rooted up by the Roots." There were tales of the kraken sinking ships by grabbing the ship in its arms and pulling

Kraken attacking a ship

3

it under. Sailors were very much afraid of meeting a kraken.

The kraken sounded like a giant creature that had many arms or tentacles. There are a couple of well-known sea creatures that have many arms or tentacles. They are the octopus and the squid. Most people know what an octopus looks like. It has a round head and body, with eight arms sticking out of the bottom. The squid is a close relative of the octopus, but it looks different. It is torpedo-shaped. All the tentacles are at one end. The squid has eight tentacles the same length, and two longer tentacles, making a total of ten.

The octopus and the squid are quite common. In many countries people eat octopus and squid. Fishermen often use them for bait. But as far as anyone knew, they were always quite small. The octopus and squid were never known to grow more than a foot or two in length. When one French scientist suggested that the kraken might really be a giant squid or octopus, other scientists laughed at him. They were sure the kraken was a myth.

It didn't matter what the scientists thought. People kept on seeing the kraken anyway. In one case, sailors came close to capturing one.

In 1861, the French ship *Alecton* was off the coast of the island of Madeira. The crew saw what looked like a kraken nearby. They decided to try and catch it. They fired shots at it. These had no effect. Finally, they wounded it with a harpoon.

They slipped a rope around the creature's tail.

The crew of the *Alecton* wanted to haul the monster back to port. It was too heavy. As they were pulling it out of the water, the tail snapped. The huge, ugly body dropped back into the sea. All the men had left from their fight was a piece of a tentacle. Soon that began to rot. It became so smelly that the crew threw it overboard.

When the *Alecton* reached port, the sailors told what had happened. But they had no evidence to

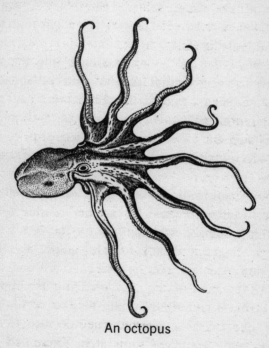

An octopus

back up their story. Very few people believed them. The story sounded too fantastic.

There were also many reports of the remains of strange creatures being washed ashore. In October, 1673, there was a tremendous storm off the coast of Ireland. When the people of the town of Dingle-l-Cosh went to the shore after the storm they found a dead monster. It had a long body, two huge eyes, and ten tentacles. People at the time thought the tentacles were horns. It was over twenty feet long.

A carnival owner named James Steward came to see the monster. He cut off two eight-foot sections of tentacle. These he exhibited in his carnival. The rest of the carcass washed back into the sea.

Steward's description of the monster sounded unreal. Educated people thought it was just carnival showmanship. The tentacles he put in his show could have been anything. Scientists of the time just didn't take James Steward's story seriously.

The scientists didn't take a lot of other stories seriously either. People from other seaside towns reported finding dead monsters on the beach like the one found at Dingle-l-Cosh. Sailors also told of seeing monsters like the one captured and then lost by the men of the *Alecton*. And the reports kept right on coming from all over the world.

By about 1870, nine years after the *Alecton* battled with a kraken, there was too much evidence to ignore. The scientists decided that the kraken was real, and that it was a giant squid. Today, the giant squid is a recognized animal. These creatures live deep in the ocean. They are rarely seen at the surface. And they are still mysterious. No one really knows how large a giant squid can grow.

The largest squid generally accepted by science was found on November 2, 1878. A fisherman named Stephen Sperring, who lived at Thimble Tickle in Newfoundland, was out in his boat with two other men. They spotted a big object in the

Giant squid beached in Newfoundland in 1877

water. At first, they thought it might be part of a wrecked ship and rowed toward it. As they got closer they found, to their horror, that the thing was very much alive.

The creature had been partly stranded in shallow water. It beat at the water with its tail and immense arms. The men were particularly frightened by the monster's eyes. The eyes looked human, but they were more than a foot and a half across. There was no doubt that they were looking at a giant squid.

Sperring and his companions were not cowards. They had seen many strange sights in the sea. But none had compared to this. They watched the creature for a while, and decided it was wounded and very weak. They were able to get close enough to it to slip a rope around its tail. They tied the other end of the rope to a tree. When the tide went out, the giant squid was left high and dry and soon died.

The fishermen did not know what to do with the monster. They cut it up and used it for dog food. But before they did, they took some rough measurements. The giant squid was at least 57 feet long from tip of tail to tip of tentacle.

The Thimble Tickle squid is the largest giant squid ever actually measured. But no one doubts that they can grow larger. Squids like the one at Thimble Tickle are washed up by accident. The really large ones may stay in the sea.

Some authorities think that the giant squid may

Giant squid attacking a man

reach a length of well over 200 feet. That would make it nearly as long as a football field!

Try to imagine what it would have been like to be a sailor in the days of wooden ships. One day you look over the side, and you see something strange and frightening in the water. It has a torpedo-shaped body, big staring eyes, and ten long tentacles. And it is longer than the boat you are on. You would surely know you had seen a monster.

So the kraken turned out to be a real monster. It was officially recognized as a giant squid over 100 years ago. Could such a large animal remain unknown today? Perhaps it could. Let us look at the squid's close relative, the octopus.

We have already said that the squid and octopus look quite different. They live differently too. The squid is streamlined. It shoots through the water at great speed. The octopus moves more slowly. It spends most of its time on the sea bottom. A bottom-dweller like the octopus would be even less likely to appear on the surface. It is also less likely that a bottom-dweller would be washed ashore.

In 1896, the rotting remains of something were washed up on the beach at St. Augustine, Florida. The remains were so badly decayed that no one was sure what it had been.

The mass was pinkish, and roughly round. Those who saw it estimated that it weighed about six tons. A local doctor named De Witt Webb examined the mass. He thought it was the remains of a giant octopus. It had no arms, but Dr. Webb' thought he found stumps where the arms had once been.

Dr. Webb cut off a few pieces of the mass and sent them, along with a description, to Professor A. E. Verrell of Yale University. Professor Verrell was an expert on sea creatures. After examining the pieces, he thought they might belong to a giant octopus. He wanted to go to Florida to see the whole mass on the beach. But he never was able to make the trip. Before any other expert on sea creatures could examine the mass, it was washed back out to sea. The evidence was lost and everybody forgot the story.

In 1957, another scientist, Dr. F. G. Wood, came across an old newspaper clipping about the giant octopus of Florida. He had never heard of it. So he decided to do some checking. He found that the pieces of the mass that had been sent to Professor Verrell still existed. They were preserved in a bottle of alcohol. The bottle had been gathering dust on a shelf at the Smithsonian Institution in Washington, D.C., since 1896.

The pieces were examined under a microscope. Under a microscope the muscles of an octopus look different from those of a squid or any other creature. These pieces had come from an octopus. If the original descriptions were correct, this creature may have measured 200 feet from arm tip to arm tip when alive. That is more than ten times as large as the largest known octopus.

Dr. Wood also remembered some stories that he had been told by fishermen in the Bahamas. The fishermen said that from time to time they had seen a giant octopus in shallow water. They had no proof of their stories. At first, Dr. Wood thought they had really seen giant squids. The fishermen insisted they knew the difference between a squid and an octopus. What they had seen was an octopus. Dr. Wood had always assumed the fishermen had made a mistake. Now he is no longer so sure. There may be a giant octopus as well as a giant squid.

So there is one monster proved to be real. The kraken is a giant squid. There is good evidence that another monster, the giant octopus, may also be real. But these are both animals of the sea. The sea is wide and deep. We know relatively little about it. We might overlook large sea animals. But surely all large land animals would have been known a long time ago. Or would they?

For centuries people had been arguing about the hairy wild man of Africa. There had been many tales about the creature. Some said it was human. Others said it was an ape. Some said that it did not exist at all.

Occasionally, skulls or pieces of hide that were supposed to be from this creature reached Europe or America. But no one was really sure what they were or where they came from. So, in 1854, the

The gorilla

Philadelphia Academy of Natural Sciences sent explorer Paul du Chaillu out to settle the question once and for all.

Du Chaillu found one of these creatures and shot it. He brought back parts of the hide and skeleton. He also had some fantastic-sounding stories to tell. He said the creature reminded him of something "half-man, half-beast." He said it thumped on its chest and roared at him. A lot of people thought that du Chaillu was exaggerating. They were suspicious of the evidence that he brought back.

Other explorers also went to central Africa. They also brought back stories about the hairy wild man that thumped its chest and roared. We now know that the "hairy wild man" was really the gorilla. But for a long time the gorilla was almost mythical.

So you can see how mythical monsters have sometimes turned out to be real. Now we are going to look at some monsters that are still thought to be mythical, but may be real.

2

SEA MONSTERS

On August 6, 1961, a sea monster was reported off the coast of Maine. One of the people who saw the monster was Donald K. Angell. He was on a ship returning from Europe to New York.

Angell said that the creature "was light in color underneath and a brownish green on top. He was 50 to 60 feet long." Angell said the monster looked rather like a giant inchworm. "We realized that here, once and for all, was a real monster!"

The monster was swimming alongside the ship. It appeared to be eating the garbage thrown overboard. Some people rushed off to get their cameras. Before they got back the monster had disappeared.

Sailors and ship passengers have reported seeing sea monsters for thousands of years. They are still reporting them today. However, sea monster re-

The legendary sea serpent

ports are not as common as they once were. One reason for this is that people now cross the oceans in large metal ships. These ships are driven by powerful engines. Up to 100 years ago, the ocean was crossed in small wooden ships. Wooden ships were powered by the wind. Large, noisy ships may frighten away sea monsters.

In fact, large ships may be dangerous to sea monsters. In 1947, crew members of the S.S. *Santa Clara* saw a sea monster off the coast of North Carolina. It was a huge serpent-like creature thrashing about in the water. The water was stained with blood. The men assumed that the creature had been hit by the ship and seriously hurt. There have been other stories of collisions between modern ships and sea monsters. The sea monsters are always the losers.

Certainly sailors today are not afraid of sea monsters. But this was not always so. At one time, sailors were terrified that a large sea monster would wreck their ships. A history book written in 1539 told of the habits of sea monsters. It said they were 200 feet long and 20 feet thick. It also said that they grabbed sailors right off the deck and ate them. Many sailors would not go into unknown regions for fear of sea monsters.

The ship-smashing, sailor-eating sea monsters are legends. Eyewitness stories of meetings with sea monsters are less sensational, but they are more believable.

The first good eyewitness account we have in writing comes from the year 1734. The witness was Hans Egede, a Protestant missionary. He was sailing in the North Atlantic near Greenland. He saw a huge monster sticking its head out of the water. He thought it was about 100 feet long. It had a pointed snout, broad paws or fins, and a wrinkled skin. It did not attack the ship. Egede was a good observer. His diaries contain good descriptions of all kinds of sea creatures. But we have no idea what this strange-looking beast was.

In August, 1746, Captain Lorenz von Ferry shot a sea monster. He was chasing it in a small boat. But the monster swam away faster than his men could row. So he loaded his gun and took a shot at it. When the shot was fired, the monster immediately dived. At the spot where the monster disappeared von Ferry found the water red. He assumed that he had wounded it.

This monster was grayish and had a head like a horse. It had large black eyes and a white mane. The head and neck had stuck out a few feet above the water. Behind the neck von Ferry could see seven or eight folds or coils. He could not estimate the length of the creature, but it was big. It was unlike any animal he had ever seen or heard of. We still don't know what it was.

One of the best sightings ever was made by the British ship *Daedalus*. On August 6, 1848, the ship was off the west coast of Africa. The lookout spotted

The sea serpent sighted from the ship **Daedalus**

what he thought was a large serpent in the water nearby. He alerted others on the ship. The creature was carefully observed by the captain and other officers and by some of the crew.

Peter M'Quhae, captain of the *Daedalus,* said they had seen "an enormous serpent, with head and shoulders kept about four feet constantly above the surface of the sea." He thought the creature was at least 60 feet long. It was moving 12 to 15 miles per hour. It came close to the ship. Captain M'Quhae said it was so close that if it had been a man he knew he would have recognized him. He watched the sea monster for over twenty minutes.

Other officers and crewmen told the same story. They gave sworn statements to the British Naval authorities. To lie to the authorities was a serious offense. Captain M'Quhae and his men had no reason to lie, and many reasons not to. They were all experienced seamen. They should have been accurate observers. There should be no possibility of a mistake.

But mistakes have been made. The sea can make men's eyes play tricks on them. Crewmen on one ship were sure they saw a sea monster. They rowed out in a small boat to get a closer look. They found that the "sea monster" was really a huge mass of seaweed. Captain J. H. Taylor once ordered his crew to fire on what he thought was a sea monster. It also turned out to be a mass of seaweed. Sometimes tree trunks have been mistaken for sea mon-

A large mass of seaweed that looked very much like a sea serpent

This "sea monster" washed ashore in Massachusetts in 1970 turned out to be the remains of a large shark

sters. Even experienced sailors have made such mistakes.

Not all sea monsters are sighted from ships. In 1817, a lot of people who lived around Gloucester Harbor in Massachusetts thought they saw a sea monster. It was reported in the harbor on many different occasions. People said it looked like a huge snake with humps on its back.

Some local amateur scientists found a small snake with humps on its back. They thought it was a baby sea serpent. It turned out to be a perfectly ordinary snake with a disease of the spine. The amateur scientists looked foolish. They didn't want to hear

21

about sea monsters after that. But they had only made a mistake about the little snake. That mistake did not explain what so many people had seen swimming in the harbor. We still don't know.

Often there are reports that a dead sea monster has been washed ashore. The remains of what looked like a sea monster were found on a beach in Massachusetts in November, 1970. Whatever it was, the thing had been dead for quite a while and was rotting. It looked like it had a long neck and small head. The body was thick and there seemed to be four small flippers. It also had a long tail. The whole carcass was about 30 feet long.

Though it looked like a sea monster, it wasn't. It was the remains of a very large shark. The shark's jaws had rotted away. Only the backbone and skull remained at the front of the carcass. That is why it looked like it had a little head and thin neck. Part

Diagram showing how a shark may look
like a sea monster—if parts of it
are missing

of the tail and underside had also rotted away.
The result was something that really did look like
a sea monster.

At other times, rotting whales or seals are mistaken for sea monsters. The carcass of a large eel
or strange fish may also be identified as the remains
of a sea monster. Sometimes strange remains are
washed away by the tides or storms before they
can be examined. In many cases we don't know
what they really were. They may have been known
animals, or they may have been sea monsters.

Along with mistakes there have been some
hoaxes. In 1845, the skeleton of a "sea monster"
was put on display. The skeleton was 114 feet long.
It had a wicked-looking pointed skull, and lots of
sharp teeth. Near the head were two large flippers.
It certainly looked like the skeleton of a sea monster.

The man who had put this monster together was
Albert Koch. He said he had dug up the bones in
Alabama. This monster was supposed to have lived
a long time ago. What Koch had found in Alabama
were the bones of ancient whales. The creatures are
called *Zeuglodons*. They died out thousands of years
ago. The real *Zeuglodon* was monstrous-looking.
But it grew only to 60 feet. That was not big enough
for Albert Koch. He put the parts of several skeletons together so he could make his monster longer.
He also added a couple of shells for front flippers.

Koch made his living by putting his skeleton on

Albert Koch's sea serpent

display. He charged admission to see it. He figured that the longer the "monster," the more people would pay. And he was right, for a while. His sea monster was very popular. But when scientists got a look at it, they could see what Koch had done. His hoax was exposed, and people would not pay to see a fake.

There are more recent hoaxes as well. In 1964, a French photographer claimed to have shot a color photograph of a sea monster. He said the picture was taken off the coast of Australia. The monster in the picture was under water. It was shaped more like a tadpole than anything else, but it was huge. It dwarfed the boat in the picture. The picture appeared in many newspapers and magazines throughout the world.

Photographs can always be faked, particularly by a person who knows about photography. It is important to know whether the photographer is some-

24

one who can be trusted. This photographer was not very trustworthy. He never paid his bills and the police were looking for him. When they finally caught up with him, he was returned to France and sent to jail. His picture of a sea monster was almost certainly a fake.

A much more puzzling case involves a sonar "picture." Sonar uses echoes instead of light to take the "picture." The device sends a sound into the water. If the sound hits a solid object, it bounces back and is picked up by the device. Through the use of sonar the distance, size, and shape of an underwater object can be determined.

Submarines often use sonar to navigate under water. Fishing boats use sonar to locate schools of fish. In nature, porpoises and whales use sonar to find their way around. Bats use it to fly in the dark.

On April 15, 1969, the American fishing boat *Mylark* was fishing for shrimp off the coast of Alaska. The ship had a new type of sonar on board. The echoes from the sonar were recorded on a long roll of paper. According to the paper, the *Mylark* had passed over a sea monster. The paper showed a "picture" of a creature with a long neck, small head, short legs, and a long tail. It was at least 150 feet long. This seemed to be proof that sea monsters really existed.

But problems soon arose. The manufacturers of the sonar equipment claimed that the reading had been faked. They said that someone had tampered with the roll of paper. The crewmen claimed that faking was not possible. By the time the manufacturers made their charge, the original roll of paper had disappeared. Without it, there is no way of settling the question. But the mere fact that the evidence has disappeared should make us very suspicious.

We don't have the remains of any sea monsters. We don't even have one single good picture of a sea monster. But we do have the statements of thousands of people. Many of them were trustworthy persons who knew the sea. Can they all have been mistaken? Are they all liars?

Captain R. J. Cringle had been called a liar so many times that he finally refused to talk about the sea monster he had seen. Captain Cringle had been commander of the steamer *Umfuli*. In the year 1900, he had been steaming toward the Cape of Good Hope at the southern tip of Africa. He saw what he called "a Monster Fish of the Serpent shape." He didn't know how long it was. He said he saw fifteen feet of the head and neck. Most of the creature was under the water. Captain Cringle said he watched the monster for half an hour. Passengers on the *Umfuli* supported his story. Yet people still said he was "seeing things."

There was one remarkable sea monster sighting during World War I. A German U-boat captain named Georg Freiherr von Forstner had just sunk a British ship. He surfaced his U-boat to inspect the wreckage. To his surprise, he found a wounded sea monster. Captain von Forstner said it looked like a 60-foot-long crocodile with a long neck. He thought it had been hurt in the explosion.

But scientists do not like to believe something from stories alone. They want better evidence. Many doubt that there really is a sea monster. But even skeptical scientists are not sure. They know that the depths of the sea have not been well explored. They admit that it would be possible for a large sea creature to remain unknown, even today. The only way we could find a large deep-sea creature is when it came to the surface. That might not happen very often.

If there is a sea monster, what might it be? Most people who believe in sea monsters think that there are several different kinds. Many descriptions make the creature sound very serpent-like. That is, they make it sound as though it were a giant sea-going snake. There are some known sea-going snakes. But these are relatively small. They also stay close to shore. But there might be larger varieties that live in the open ocean.

Many sea monster sightings mention fins or flippers. The descriptions make the sea monsters sound like sea-going reptiles from the age of the dinosaurs. The dinosaurs lived over 70 million years ago. At that time there were many huge reptiles that looked like sea monsters. Could some of them have survived? Some people think so.

Identifying sea monsters as reptiles—and snakes are reptiles too—brings up a problem. Reptiles are cold-blooded. They need warm temperatures to survive. All the reptiles we know of live in warm areas or hibernate during the winter. Yet many sea monsters have been sighted in northern waters. No reptile should be able to survive under those conditions.

That brings up mammals. Mammals are warm-blooded. Mammals like seals and whales do live in northern waters. Sea mammals also grow very large. The blue whale is the largest known living thing, ever. It is much bigger than the biggest dinosaur. A Belgian naturalist, Bernard Heuvelmans, suggests there are several kinds of unknown sea mammals. He thinks these account for most of the sea monster sightings.

Some think that there may be giant eels in the sea. All known eels start life as tiny larvae. In the 1930s, Dr. Anton Bruun, a Danish biologist, caught a six-foot-long eel larvae in the sea. If that eel larvae had grown like most others, the adult would have been well over 100 feet long. A monster indeed!

This is all guesswork. We shall never really know whether there is one sea monster, or several, or none at all, until we have better evidence. We need more than sightings. We need a good close-up photograph of one. Or better still, motion pictures. But best of all would be to catch a sea monster. Dr. Bruun thought that catching a sea monster is possible, but that it required a special technique. He said, "I have no doubt that such a monster could be caught."

Perhaps one was nearly caught. In the 1930s, research scientists were "fishing" in very deep waters. They were just trying to see what they might come up with. At 1,200 feet they hooked into something —large, active, and very strong. Whatever it was, it was strong enough to bend a three-foot iron hook and escape. That was really the big one that got away.

3

THE LOCH NESS MONSTER

The most famous modern monster comes from Scotland. It is the Loch Ness monster. People call it "Nessie" for short.

Let us set the scene. "Loch" is a Scottish word for lake. But Loch Ness does not look like any lake you have ever seen. It is 27 miles long, and only a mile wide. It is also very deep, over 700 feet deep in some places. There are few beaches. In most places the sides of the loch go straight down for hundreds of feet.

The waters of Loch Ness are cold and dark. Under water a diver can see only a few feet, even with a strong light. There are strong currents that make swimming dangerous. People have drowned in the loch and their bodies have never been found.

Storms are sudden and unexpected at Loch Ness. Even going out in a boat can be dangerous.

Thousands of years ago, Loch Ness opened directly into the sea. But the land rose, and the loch was cut off from the sea. Now, the only connection between the loch and the sea is the little river Ness.

Loch Ness is in northern Scotland. It is a region called the Highlands. The Highland Scots were a wild and war-like people. They were also great storytellers. They told tales of monsters, ghosts, and demons. According to the Scots, practically every loch had a monster or two.

But the story about the monster in Loch Ness was special. It had been written down nearly 1,500 years ago. At that time, a great holy man named St. Columba came to Scotland. It was his mission to convert the pagan Scots to Christianity. He came to be regarded as the patron saint of Scotland.

One day St. Columba was standing by the edge of Loch Ness. A man was swimming nearby. Suddenly the monster rose up out of the water. The terrified swimmer struggled to get back to shore. St. Columba held up his hand and ordered the monster not to touch the swimmer. The monster sank back into the water.

This story was included in St. Columba's official biography. It was read and reread in churches for hundreds of years. The Highland Scots may have doubted a lot of the monster stories they heard. But they did not doubt this story of the Loch Ness monster.

Until about fifty years ago, Loch Ness was an isolated place. It was rarely visited by outsiders. In 1933, the government began building a road around the loch. Then the outside world first began to hear of the Loch Ness monster.

A man named Alex Campbell worked at the loch for many years. He first saw the monster in 1934. He said it had a long thin neck and a small head. It looked rather like a snake. Sticking out of the water behind the head was a large hump. The head and neck were about six feet long. The hump was 30 feet long. A good part of the creature remained under water. Whatever it was, it was big.

Photograph showing "humps" of the
Loch Ness monster

Campbell also wrote for a local paper. In his article he called the thing he had seen a "monster." He didn't know what else to call it. The name stuck.

Later that same year, a man named Arthur Grant was riding his motorcycle on the road near the loch. It was night. In the beam of his headlight he saw something cross the road. It looked like nothing he had ever seen before. It had a long, thin neck, fat body, short legs, and a long tapering tail. It was also very large. Mr. Grant turned his motorcycle around and rode quickly the other way.

In the summer of 1934, Kenneth Wilson came to Loch Ness on vacation. Mr. Wilson was a surgeon from London. Early one evening he saw something strange in the water. He had his camera with him and took a picture. The picture showed what looked like a long, thin neck and small head coming out of the water.

The picture was published in newspapers throughout the world. So were the stories of people who said they had seen the monster. The Loch Ness monster was no longer a local legend. It had become world famous.

According to the story of St. Columba and the monster, it was a pretty vicious beast. It tried to attack a swimmer. But in recent years no one has reported being attacked by the monster. It seems to be very peaceful and shy. Most people who believe in it are not afraid of it. A few people who have sighted the monster while they were in a small

The London surgeon's famous photograph
of the Loch Ness monster

boat on the loch said they were afraid. The monster
looked large enough to tip over the boat. But, in
general, Nessie is not a frightening creature.

Since 1934, thousands of persons have reported
seeing the Loch Ness monster. Many people have
taken photographs of what they thought was the
monster. Some movies of the monster have also
been made.

The best motion pictures were taken in 1960.
The photographer was Tim Dinsdale. Dinsdale had
come to Loch Ness to look for the monster. He had
spent many hours staring at the water without seeing
anything. Finally, he saw something moving in the
water. It was on the other side of the loch, so he

couldn't see it too well. But he took motion pictures of it anyway.

The quality of the Dinsdale film was poor. The object looked like a spot moving through the water. For years no one paid much attention to the film. In 1965, the film was given to photographic experts of the Royal Air Force (RAF). They examined it carefully, frame by frame.

At first, the experts' report on the Dinsdale film was kept secret. But news of it soon leaked out, and it was made public. The report caused a sensation. The experts concluded that the thing in the film was probably alive. They estimated it could be over 90 feet long. If the report was correct, Tim Dinsdale had filmed the Loch Ness monster.

Not everyone agreed with the RAF experts. Some said that Dinsdale had photographed a motorboat. The film was too fuzzy for anyone to be really sure. Those who believed in the monster were encouraged, but they needed more evidence. Regular expeditions were organized to try to get better pictures of the monster.

If the Loch Ness monster exists, it does not come to the surface very often. It would seem that the best thing to do would be to try to photograph it under the water. But that is not as easy as it sounds. Remember, we said the water of Loch Ness is very dark. This is because the water is filled with a substance called peat. Trying to take a photograph under water is like trying to take a photograph in

Searching for the monster at Loch Ness

a thick fog. A diver would have to be almost on top of an object before he could get a picture of it. Besides, divers don't like going into the waters of the loch.

In 1970, two small submarines were brought to Loch Ness. They were equipped with powerful searchlights and cameras. It was hoped that they could explore the loch and find the monster. But the submarines could not operate effectively in the dark water. The project was a failure.

Monster hunters had more success with an automatic underwater camera. It was rigged up to go off if something passed near it. A powerful light would flash at the same time. One photograph showed what looked like a flipper and part of the body of a large animal.

Sonar was also used to try and track the monster. Several different teams of sonar operators detected what they thought could be the monster. But sonar is not perfect. Readings can be misinterpreted. A school of fish swimming close together can produce the same sort of reading as a single large object. Once again, the evidence was interesting, but there were still plenty of doubters.

Why do so many people, particularly scientists, doubt the existence of the Loch Ness monster? First, we must realize there cannot be a *single* Loch Ness monster. If there were only one, it would have to have lived since the time of St. Columba. That is nearly 1,500 years. An immortal monster is unthinkable.

So there must be a colony of them. It's hard to imagine how a single monster has been so successful at avoiding photographers. How could a colony of them be so hard to find?

Photograph taken in 1955 at Loch Ness. The castle tower is sixty-four feet above the water. It can be compared to the size of the "thing" in the water.

What happens to them when they die? One would think a dead monster would float to the surface. The remains of one should have been washed onto the land. Yet no dead monster has been found. Not even a bone has ever turned up.

What would they eat? There are salmon, eels, and other fish in Loch Ness. But a colony of large creatures would eat an enormous number of fish. Many scientists do not think there are that many fish in Loch Ness.

What about the pictures and the thousands of

sightings? Most of them are mistakes, say the doubters. Even supporters admit that it is easy to make mistakes. Some of the sightings and pictures are also faked. Once a man brought a stuffed hippopotamus foot to Loch Ness. He used it to make footprints at the edge of the loch. At first, people thought they had found footprints of the monster. Then they found the stuffed hippopotamus foot, and knew they had been fooled.

But can all of the sightings and all of the pictures have been mistakes or fakes? People who have studied the monster for years say no. They cannot explain why no remains of the monster have been found. They cannot explain what the monster eats. But they say there is too much evidence to ignore.

Those who believe in the monster say it came from the sea—that it is sort of an inland sea monster. Thousands of years ago the creatures lived in the open ocean. At that time, Loch Ness was open to the sea. The "monsters" could swim in and out of the loch. Then the land rose. Loch Ness was separated from the sea, and a group of the creatures was trapped. They have been living in Loch Ness ever since.

What kind of animal might the Loch Ness monster be? One popular idea is that it is a gigantic reptile. When the dinosaurs lived on the land, giant reptiles lived in the sea. That was over 70 million years ago. As far as we know, none of those giants are still alive. One of these giant reptiles was called a "plesiosaur." It had a small head, long thin neck, fat body, flippers, and a long tapering tail. These creatures have been called "swan dragons." They looked just the way many people have described the Loch Ness monster. Some monster-watchers think a small colony of plesiosaurs is living in Loch Ness.

Another suggestion is that the animal might be a mammal. Mammals are warm-blooded. They would be better adapted for living in the cold waters of Loch Ness. When we talked about sea monsters, we said that reptiles were cold-blooded. They do not live well in cold climates. Some descriptions of the Loch Ness monster make it sound like a seal with a long neck. Seals are mammals, and they can grow very large. One type reaches 20 feet in length. No seal that we know of has a long neck. But there is no reason why one couldn't have a long neck.

A close relative of the seal is the sea cow. A century ago, a type of sea cow lived off the coast of Alaska. It grew to a length of 35 feet—truly monster size. This type of sea cow was wiped out by hunters. Still, we know that sea cows can grow very large.

Smaller sea cows still live in southern waters. There is something very interesting about them. They are very shy and hard to see. They spend almost all of their time under the water. When they come to the surface to breathe, they only stick the tips of their nostrils above the water. Many people have lived near sea cows and have never seen them. This makes some form of long-necked sea cow a good candidate for the Loch Ness monster. If Nessie exists, it is also very shy.

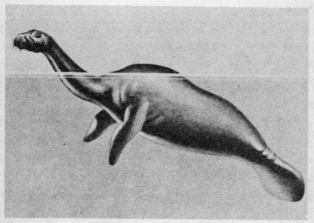

One scientist suggested that the Loch Ness monster might be a giant sea cow with a long neck. It would look like this.

The Loch Ness monster might be an invertebrate. Invertebrates are animals without backbones. The most common invertebrates are insects and are quite small. But squids are also invertebrates. As we have seen, squids can grow to truly monstrous sizes.

There is one type of invertebrate that fits the description of the Loch Ness monster. It is the slug. The slug looks like a snail without a shell. Like the snail, it has two antennae on top of its head. Some observers have reported that the Loch Ness monster has two antenna-like projections on its head. There are a variety of slugs that live in the sea. None of them grow very large. But for a long time no one thought that squids grew very large either.

Monsters have been spotted in other Scottish lochs. A number of people have reported seeing a large, strange creature in Loch Morar. This creature has been called Morag. There have been monster sightings in lakes in Ireland, Sweden, and Russia too.

Many monster reports have come from a large lake in Western Canada. The lake is called Lake Okanagan. It is located in the province of British Columbia. The Indians who lived near the lake had legends about a monster called Ogopogo. In recent years others have reported seeing Ogopogo. Ogopogo is supposed to have a long neck and humps like the Loch Ness monster. Some people have also reported that it has whiskers like a walrus.

Do any of these creatures really exist? Most scientists doubt that they do. The scientists say that if they did, there would be more evidence. But the thousands and thousands of people who have seen the Loch Ness monster, or Ogopogo, or the others say they do exist. There is only one thing that we can say for sure: the search will continue.

4

THE YETI

The highest mountains in the world are the Himalayas of Asia. For many years there had been stories of a strange creature that lived high in the Himalayas. The creature was very large—as much as nine feet tall—and walked on two legs. It was covered with hair, was very strong, and might be dangerous. This thing was known by many names. Some people called it the Abominable Snowman. But the most common name was the Yeti.

The Sherpas are people who live at the base of the high mountains. They are excellent mountain climbers. They have often guided other climbers and explorers. Travelers in the mountains would sometimes see strange footprints in the snow. They would ask their Sherpa guides what the footprints were. The Sherpas would reply that they were

Yeti prints. The Sherpas often had tales of friends or relatives who had seen a Yeti.

Prince Peter of Greece visited the Himalayas one time. He didn't see a Yeti, but he heard many Yeti stories. He was told of one village that was bothered by a Yeti. The creature came down from the mountains and stole the villagers' food. The villagers decided to catch it. One night they put out a bowl of strong liquor. The Yeti drank the liquor and fell asleep, so the villagers were able to capture it. But when it woke up, it broke its ropes and ran away.

Stories like this did not get much attention. The account that really got things going was published in 1925. It was written by N. A. Tombazi, a photographer with a British geographical expedition.

Tombazi was high in the mountains. His guide told him there was something strange in the distance. He tried to see what the guide was talking about. For a moment, he could see nothing because of the glare from the snow and ice. Then he saw "it."

"It" was a figure. Tombazi said it had the outline of a human figure. It walked upright. Occasionally, it stooped down to pull at some bushes growing at the edge of the snowfield. As far as Tombazi could tell, it wore no clothes. He watched it for about a minute. Then it disappeared into a patch of bushes. He didn't have a chance to take a picture. He didn't even have time to look at it carefully with binoculars.

A couple of hours later, Tombazi returned to the

spot where he had seen the creature. It was gone. But its footprints were clearly marked in the snow. The prints were only six or seven inches long, smaller than a man's. But they were similar in shape. Tombazi said, "The marks of five distinct toes and of the instep were perfectly clear . . ." Who was walking around the Himalayan snowfields without clothes or shoes? Or what was walking around?

Tombazi was a man with an excellent reputation. No one has ever suggested that he lied or exaggerated. But he only had a fleeting glimpse of the figure. And he never took a picture of the footprints.

A number of other Westerners have reported seeing the Yeti. But it is hard to put much stock in most of these reports. Sometimes they are second-hand or third-hand. In another case, a report is contained in a book that has so many obvious falsehoods that it is hard to believe anything the author says.

Aside from Tombazi, there is only one other reliable sighting reported by a Westerner. It took place in 1970. The man who saw the creature was Don Whillans, a well-known mountain climber. Whillans didn't get too good a look at the thing. It was night, and he saw it only in the moonlight. It was a considerable distance away. Whillans said it was "bounding along on all fours." It looked to him like a large ape. The next day he went to the spot where he had seen the creature and took a photograph of the tracks it left in the snow.

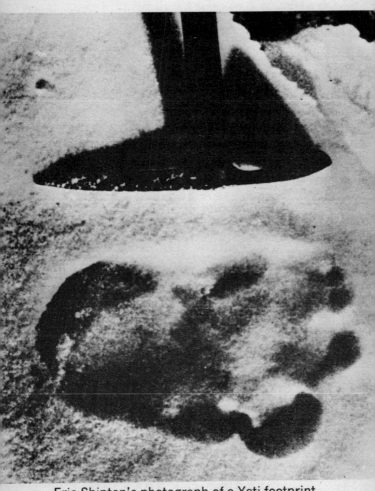

Eric Shipton's photograph of a Yeti footprint,
compared in size to the head of an ice axe

Unfortunately, the photograph isn't very good. No one can tell whether it shows tracks of an unknown animal or not.

The best photograph of a Yeti footprint was taken in 1951. The photographer was Eric Shipton, one of the most famous mountain climbers of his day. Shipton was in the Himalayas scouting Mount Everest. He was one of those who prepared the way for the first successful climb of the world's highest mountain. Shipton and his companion, Michael Ward, were crossing the Menlung glacier. Late in the afternoon, they found a set of fresh tracks in the snow. They followed the tracks for about a mile.

Shipton picked out what he thought was the clearest of the prints. He took photographs of it. In one picture he used his companion's ice axe for size comparison. In the other photograph, Ward put his boot near the print. The print was bigger than the boot and nearly as big as the axe.

The photographs are very clear. They show a print that looks roughly human or ape-like. The print shows four toes—a large big toe and three smaller toes. It does not look like the footprint of any known animal. The Shipton photograph was the best piece of evidence ever presented in favor of the Yeti. Many people think it still is the best. The photograph made the subject of the Yeti respectable. Scientists did not necessarily believe in the Yeti, but they were more willing to discuss it.

Several expeditions set out to find the Yeti. But the members of the expeditions failed to photograph a Yeti, or even see one. They brought back some photographs of footprints. But these were not as good as the photographs taken by Shipton. Experts looking at the photographs thought that they were the footprints of known animals.

In 1960, a really large expedition set out to find the Yeti. The expedition was headed by Sir Edmund Hillary. Hillary was the man who, along with Sherpa Tenzing Norgay, first climbed Mount Everest. He was very famous. Another member of the expedition was Marlin Perkins. He is an American zoologist. For years, Perkins has been the host of a series of television shows on animals. He was also well known. There has never been a better publicized monster-hunting expedition. And as far as the Yeti's reputation was concerned, it was a disaster.

The Hillary expedition did not find the Yeti. That was bad enough. The expedition did not find any evidence that there *was* a Yeti. That was worse. But worst of all was what Sir Edmund Hillary said when he came back. He said he was now sure that there was no such thing as a Yeti. He then proceeded to pick apart all the evidence that had ever been presented in favor of the Yeti.

Other travelers had said that people who lived in the Himalayas worshipped the Yeti. They said that the scalps and skins and bones of Yetis were kept in monasteries. The people regarded these remains as sacred objects. They rarely showed them to outsiders, and never would allow them to be taken away. There were a few photographs of what were supposed to be Yeti scalps. The Yeti is said to have a pointed head. The scalps looked rather like pointed fur caps. It was hard to tell much from the photographs.

Hillary not only got a look at one of these Yeti scalps, but was able to take it with him. He brought it back to America. It was closely examined by scientists. Hairs from it were looked at under the microscope. It turned out to be just what it looked like—a pointed fur cap. It had been made from goat skin.

He looked at some Yeti skins, and said they were really bear skins. The Yeti bones were the bones of known animals.

The footprints were not so easy to explain. But Hillary reminded those who believed in the Yeti of something important about footprints in the snow. After a print is made, the snow may melt a bit during the day. It will refreeze at night and melt a bit more during the next day. This melting and freezing will change the shape of a print. After a few days a familiar footprint may look very strange. Several small footprints close together will resemble one large print.

Hillary didn't believe the Sherpa stories either. He said that Sherpas have vivid imaginations. They

Stamps supposedly showing drawings of the Yeti.
They were issued by the tiny kingdom of
Bhutan in 1966.

believe in all sorts of mountain spirits. The Yeti was just another one of them, Hillary said.

Another member of Hillary's expedition pointed out that Sherpas are also very polite. A traveler may ask a Sherpa about the Yeti. The Sherpa does not want to disappoint the traveler, so he tells him something about a Yeti. It does not matter to the Sherpa that the story is not true. He is simply doing what he believes is the polite thing. It is the same with footprints. The traveler sees strange marks in the snow. He asks the Sherpa if they are the footprints of the Yeti. The Sherpa agrees that they are. Once again, the Sherpa is only being polite.

What about the sightings? Hillary thought that most of the people who said they saw a Yeti were really seeing a bear standing on its hind legs. Most of the Yeti footprints were really bear prints, he said.

Another animal that might be mistaken for the Yeti was the langur, a type of monkey. Some kinds of langurs are sometimes found high in the mountains. But the langur is only a few feet long. Most reports say the Yeti is huge—eight or nine feet tall, at least. Doubters say that sizes are very hard to estimate in the mountains. The snow often confuses people. Besides, they say there have not been that many sightings.

Some of the Yeti footprints and sightings may have been caused by men. Religious hermits sometimes live in the high Himalayas. They can become adapted to the cold. These men have been known to walk around in the snow without shoes. Sometimes they wear little or no clothes. The cold does not seem to bother them.

But what if a traveler saw one of these hermits at a distance? Or what if he found a trail of naked footprints? Would the traveler believe they had been made by a man? He would more likely think that the Yeti was responsible.

Hillary's explanations made a lot of people angry. They said he was being unfair, and too negative. They accused him of being bitter because he did not find the Yeti himself. But Sir Edmund Hillary stuck by his opinions. And he still sticks by them.

After the Hillary expedition, interest in the Yeti declined. But it did not disappear. It was, after all, only one man's opinion, even if that man was the "Conqueror of Everest."

Yeti supporters admit that some of their evidence may have been wrong. But they insist there is too much of it to be brushed aside. They say that experienced mountaineers can tell the difference between fresh footprints and footprints that have melted. Many of the Yeti prints have been fresh, they say.

They also point out that the Sherpas know the mountains better than anyone else. If the Sherpas believe in Yetis, then there must be something to the belief.

Those who believe in the Yeti have different

ideas about what it might be. One popular idea is that it is an unknown giant ape. Fossils of a giant ape have been found in China. When alive, this creature would have been larger than the largest gorilla. It could easily account for the Yeti stories—if it is still alive. But is it? We have no solid evidence that it is. All the fossil remains are thousands of years old.

There are no known large apes in China today. Chinese records speak of large apes living in China just a few hundred years ago. The apes may have died out in the populated areas of China. But perhaps a small number of them still exist in the mountains. It is possible that even a large animal could remain hidden for years in the Himalayas.

But some Yeti supporters have an even more sensational idea. They say that the Yeti is some unknown form of primitive, man-like creature. The Yeti has been called a "missing link" between ape and man.

To find a large unknown ape in the Himalayas would be remarkable. To find a large unknown man, or near-man, would be absolutely startling. Yet the idea is not a crazy one. We now know that a considerable variety of man-like creatures once existed.

For many years, there have been rumors about "wild men" in Russia. These wild men are called the Almas. They are supposed to live in various remote mountain ranges in Russia. They have occasionally been sighted by Russian scientists.

In 1957, the Russian scientist, A. G. Pronin, was in the Pamir Mountains. One evening he saw a strange man-like figure on a cliff top. The figure was about a quarter of a mile away. It was hunched over, had long arms, and was covered with reddish-gray hair. A few days later he saw it again. Local villagers said they knew about this type of creature. They called it a "wild man."

An old Tibetan drawing of a "wild man" that some people think may be the Yeti.

Two years later, another scientist led an expedition to the same area. The aim of the expedition was to see if the scientists could find out anything more about the wild man. The expedition did not find the wild man. What it did find were some stone tools and cave drawings. It also found evidence that people had been living in some of the mountain caves. All of this indicated that there might be some sort of primitive human being in the Russian mountains.

But the Russians have not presented any physical evidence that these Almas exist. They have not even been very cooperative about supplying information. Some Russian scientists are a bit embarrassed by such stories. They do not think the Almas exist.

The Almas are usually described as being shorter than an ordinary person. The Yeti is almost always described as being larger. It is unlikely that they are both the same creature. But if one unknown creature can exist in the mountains, why not another?

In fact, many of those who believe in the Yeti say there must be several different kinds. Descriptions and footprints are often very different. The Sherpas and other mountain people also talk about a number of man-like creatures. The Yeti is only the most famous of them.

Is there one Yeti, several, or none at all? The question remains unsettled.

5

BIGFOOT

It is easy to believe in monsters living in the sea, or in the Himalaya Mountains, or even at the bottom of Loch Ness. But how about a monster in California, or Washington State, or Minnesota, or Missouri, or Florida? Monster stories in our own back yard are somehow harder to believe. Yet, right now, there is more interest in an American monster than any other.

This monster has been called by many names. In Canada, it is known as the Sasquatch. But the name that has become the most popular is Bigfoot. Bigfoot is sort of an American Yeti or Abominable Snowman. In fact, it has been suggested that the Yeti may have migrated to America from Asia. A few thousand years ago, Alaska and Russia were attached. The Indians came to North America by

Rene Dahinden, a veteran Bigfoot hunter, stands beside an eight-foot-tall wood carving of Bigfoot in Willow Creek, California.

walking across this land bridge. The Yeti may have come the same way.

There are some old Indian legends about a big, hairy, man-like creature. Most of these legends come from northern California, Washington, Oregon, and the western coast of Canada. Sightings of such a creature had occasionally been reported. Many people had claimed to have found giant footprints. Photographs of these footprints sometimes appeared in newspapers.

No one came up with really solid evidence that Bigfoot existed. But there were so many stories that one could get a picture of the creature. Bigfoot was usually described as tall—anywhere from six to nine feet. It walked on two legs, like a man. It was broad, probably weighing over 300 pounds when full-grown. It was completely covered with short dark hair, except for the face, which was bare. Those who got close enough to look at its face said it looked ape-like, yet strangely human. Some reports said that Bigfoot was shy. Others said they had been attacked by the creature.

Interest in Bigfoot continued to grow. More people went out looking for it. People who believe in monsters thought it would only be a matter of time until solid evidence turned up.

Then, on October 20, 1967, a couple of monster hunters apparently struck pay dirt. Roger Patterson had been looking for Bigfoot for years. He firmly believed in the creature. He had even written a book on the subject. But he had never seen one. That was not his fault. He had tracked down every Bigfoot lead. He had often gone into the woods where Bigfoot was supposed to live.

He had already searched the area around Bluff Creek, California, several times. There had been many Bigfoot reports from the region. In 1967, he went back with his friend, Bob Gimlin.

The country is rugged, and there are few roads. Patterson and Gimlin traveled mostly on horseback. Patterson always tried to keep a motion picture camera loaded with color film close at hand, just in case.

At 3:30 in the afternoon of October 20, the pair rode into a clearing. At the other side of the clearing they saw Bigfoot. The creature was very large and covered with shiny, dark fur.

Patterson jumped from his horse and started taking pictures. Bigfoot turned toward the camera. Then it walked rapidly away. It took long strides and swung its arms. The creature was gone before Patterson had a chance to reload his camera. Patterson estimated that the creature was about eight feet tall and weighed several hundred pounds.

After the film was developed, Patterson and Gimlin held a news conference. They passed out stills from the film to waiting reporters. The photographs created a sensation. Newspapers all over the country carried the stories. Magazines followed with more detailed accounts. There were radio and television interviews.

Gimlin soon faded into the background, but Patterson continued to travel around the country showing his Bigfoot film and giving lectures. He was an extremely popular lecturer until his death in 1972.

This is the sort of proof we have been looking for all along—good clear film of a monster in action. So, can we say for sure that Bigfoot exists? Well, not exactly. The problem is that some of the people who have seen the film think that the creature in it is a fake. They say it looks like a man in a monkey suit.

One of the scientists who saw the film was John Napier, an expert on monkeys and apes. For a while, it appeared as if Napier had said the film was genuine. But all he really said was that he could not prove it was a fake. Later, he explained, "I could not see the zipper, and I still can't." Napier, however, is still interested in Bigfoot. He is convinced that there must be *something* behind all the stories.

If the creature in the film isn't a man in costume, it could be. If there is no way to prove it is a fake, there is no way to prove it is real either. To prove the existence of this monster, we are still going to need better evidence.

There are an awful lot of people who claim to have seen Bigfoot. There is even one man who

Bigfoot exists still don't believe the story. It is
nge story. But it is not the strangest ever told
about Bigfoot.

The prize for the strangest story may go to
prospector Fred Beck. In 1924, Beck and four
companions were hunting for gold on Mount St.
Helens in Washington State. They found a promis-
ing-looking place to dig, in a canyon high in the
mountains. They built a cabin for themselves and
started digging.

Something began robbing their camp. First, they
thought it was a bear. But they found no bear
pawprints. What they did find were enormous foot-
nts. Except for the size, the prints looked human.

he men took to carrying their rifles every-
ere. One day two of the men thought they saw
huge, ape-like creature looking at them. They
th fired, but missed. The next day Fred Beck
ed at one of the creatures. He didn't miss. But
body fell off the cliff and into a creek below.
never found.

rospectors returned to their cabin. That
were awakened by a loud thumping
of of the cabin. It sounded as though
ere throwing large rocks at the cabin.
exactly what was happening. A crowd
res had come to the cabin and were
it down.

attack lasted for several hours. The men
d at the creatures through chinks in the cabin

Frame from another film supposedly showing
Bigfoot, this time high on a rocky ledge

wall. But they were shooting in the dark. Just before dawn the creatures gave up and went away. The five prospectors did not hang around to see what was going to happen next. They got off the mountain and back to town as soon as they could.

When they told their story, a search party was organized. The group returned to the cabin. They found the large footprints, and some blood. But the creatures were gone.

That is the story as Fred Beck told it. There is no way to check it out. A lot of people simply don't believe it. But a lot of people do. The canyon in which the attack was supposed to have taken place was named Ape Canyon. That name is still in use today. The name, Bigfoot, was unknown to Fred Beck. He had called the creatures "giant apes." Even today, hopeful monster hunters go to Ape Canyon looking for the beasts.

While no Bigfoot has been seen in Ape Canyon for a long time, they continue to be seen elsewhere. In 1969, Verlin Herrington was driving along a road in Washington State one night. As he rounded a bend, he saw a creature standing in the road. It had been momentarily blinded by his headlights. It was large and hairy and stood about eight feet tall. At first, Herrington thought it was a bear standing on two legs. But, on closer examination, he decided it looked human. It must have been Bigfoot.

In 1971, Richard Brown, a teacher, was hunting near Dallas, Oregon. Through the scope of his rifle, he saw something he had not been hunting for. It was a tall, hairy, ape-like creature crossing a meadow. Bigfoot again. Brown watched the thing for a few minutes, but didn't shoot. In the next few days, a dozen other people reported seeing the monster in the same area.

Many hunters have reported seeing Bigfoot. But they rarely shoot at it. William Roe's reaction was typical. In October, 1955, he said he met Bigfoot while hunting in the Canadian province of British Columbia. Roe was just a few feet from it. He had his rifle in his hand. He decided not to shoot because it looked "too human." He thought he would never forgive himself.

Most of the reports of Bigfoot come from the Pacific Northwest. Not all of them do, however. In November, 1966, six young men were hunting deer in Wisconsin when they encountered Bigfoot. Once again, they did not shoot.

In July, 1972, armed men poured into the woods near the town of East Peoria, Illinois. They were looking for a Bigfoot-type of creature that had been reported there. They didn't shoot Bigfoot, but one of the hunters shot himself in the leg. A little while later the same sort of creature was reported near Cairo, Illinois.

There were several sightings of a big, hairy monster in Missouri in 1971. The press there called the thing Mo-Mo—short for Missouri Monster. But, from the descriptions, it was Bigfoot. There

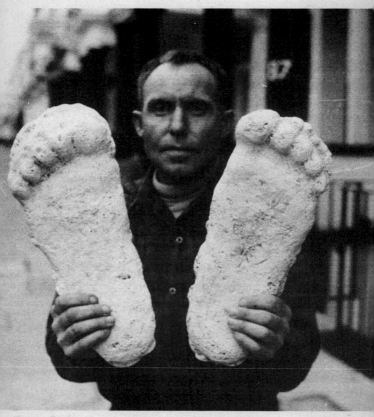

Rene Dahinden holds plaster casts of the footprints
left by the creature in the Patterson-Gimlin film.

were a large number of monster reports in Florida in 1973. There the creature was called the Skunk Ape. Some people said they were close enough to it to smell it. It smelled awful.

This is nowhere near a complete list of sightings. New sightings are reported from around the country every month. But scientists want more than stories of what people say they saw. They want solid evidence. What do we have? First, we have the footprints. Enormous footprints have been reported very often. That is, in fact, how Bigfoot got its name.

A good set of footprints was found by Jerry Crew, a bulldozer operator. In 1957, he was helping to build a road near Bluff Creek, California. Ten years later, Roger Patterson was to shoot his famous Bigfoot film in the same area. One day, Crew found enormous footprints in the soft earth near the construction camp. He made a plaster cast of one of the prints. Then he was photographed holding the cast. It stretched from his collar to his belt. Many others have made plaster casts of prints or taken photographs of them.

Unfortunately, footprints can be faked. On a television special on monsters, one man showed how he faked Bigfoot prints. He simply attached pieces of wood, shaped like a huge human foot, to his boots. Then he ran around in the snow. These fake prints fooled a lot of people. But can all of the reported footprints have been faked? We do not know.

The best piece of evidence would be a living Bigfoot. The next best piece of evidence would be a dead one. In 1968, a dead Bigfoot, or something very like it, was supposed to be on display in a Midwestern carnival. It was frozen in a block of ice. People had to pay an admission fee to see it. When they got into the tent, they couldn't see very much. But there was something in the ice. The "something" looked vaguely human, hairy, and large.

The exhibit attracted the attention of Ivan Sanderson. Sanderson was a biologist and enthusiastic supporter of the Bigfoot idea. He decided to examine the thing in the ice more closely. At the time, Bernard Heuvelmans, a Belgian biologist who was interested in monsters was visiting Sanderson. They both went to the Minnesota farm where the exhibit was being stored.

The two biologists were not allowed to melt the ice to examine the thing closely. But looking through the ice, they decided that it was real. They said so in public. Then the fun began. Sanderson got in touch with the Smithsonian Institution in Washington. Scientists there agreed to examine it. At first, it seemed as though the carnival man who owned the thing was going to let them do it. But he began raising objections. The Smithsonian scientists dropped their offer. The carnival man then began to tell all sorts of different stories about where he got the thing and who owned it.

69

Finally, a company in Hollywood that made monster models for the movies admitted that they had made this one too. The Minnesota Iceman, as the creature came to be called, was a fake.

Where do we stand with Bigfoot? The case for it rests on a large number of sightings and many footprints. The case against it is mainly that we do not have better evidence. It is hard to imagine how such a large and strange-looking creature could be so hard to find—particularly when people have been tramping all over the woods looking for it. But it is also hard to imagine how all those sightings and footprints could be mistakes or hoaxes.

Scientists thought the kraken was a myth. It turned out to be a giant squid. True, a lot of mythical animals have turned out to be just that—mythical. No one has ever found a unicorn or a mermaid. No one now seriously believes that such creatures ever existed. Perhaps Bigfoot will turn out to be more like the kraken than the unicorn. Perhaps some of the other monsters we have talked about in this book will turn out to be real too.

6

DRAGONS EVERYWHERE

Everyone knows what dragons look like. They look like big lizards that have wings and can breathe fire. They are also very evil. When they are not guarding their treasure, they are menacing fair maidens or fighting with brave knights. Right? Wrong—because there are many kinds of dragons. People all over the world have believed in dragons. It is the most common monster in the world.

The dragon just described appears in fairy tales from Europe. But in China there are other kinds of dragons. These also look a bit like large lizards. But they do not always breathe fire, and they never have wings. They are also not evil. In fact, the Chinese consider dragons as symbols of good luck. Dragon models are used in Chinese New Year's celebrations.

Traditional fire-breathing dragon being attacked
by a knight in spiked armor

And there are other sorts of dragons. Some have only two legs. But a long time ago, dragons did not have any legs at all. They looked just like giant snakes. The fact is that they *were* giant snakes.

These were the dragons the ancient Romans knew. The Romans used their Latin word, *draco,* to describe a giant snake. They had many wild tales to tell about the *draco*. They said that it lived in trees and was so large it could kill and eat an elephant. Others said that it had a poisonous breath and could kill by just breathing on a victim.

The stories sound fantastic, but there is some truth behind them. In India and Africa there are very large snakes. The python is the best-known large snake. Some grow to 30 feet or more. They hide in trees. When an animal walks under the tree, the giant snake will drop on it. These snakes kill their victims by squeezing them to death. They eat small deer and pigs—not elephants—but this is probably how that story got started.

There are many snakes that have poisonous bites. The cobra is a type of snake that can spit deadly poison. This may have started the story about the *draco* having a poisonous breath. This may also be how the idea of a fire-breathing dragon began.

The word *draco* became our word "dragon." For hundreds of years, dragons were shown as huge snakes. When the Bible was translated into English, the words "dragon" and "serpent" or "snake"

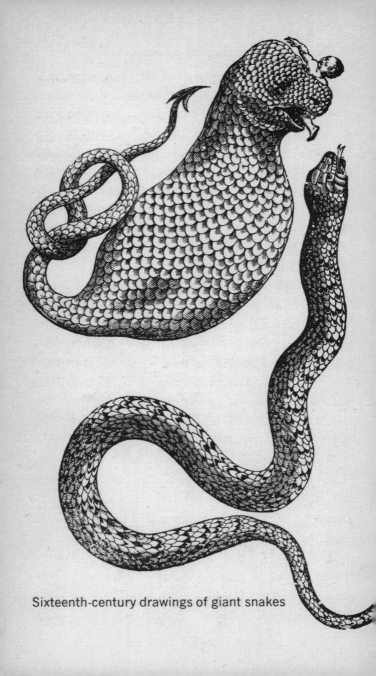

Sixteenth-century drawings of giant snakes

often meant the same thing. The Devil is often called a dragon or a serpent.

So, really, the dragon is a giant snake. But where did we get the idea that dragons had wings and legs. No one seems to know the answer to that question. In the year 1557, five "baby dragons" were on display in Paris. They were dead, of course, and very small. But they had wings and legs. However, they only had two legs. We only have descriptions of these "dragons." The actual specimens have disappeared.

We do not know what these baby dragons really were, but we can make a good guess. They were man-made monsters. Somebody had probably attached bat wings to a dead lizard. Then they cut off two of the lizard's legs to make it look stranger. This sort of thing was done all the time. Sailors would occasionally bring back "mermaids" from China. These "Chinese mermaids" were the top half of a monkey sewn to the bottom half of a fish. They sold for high prices. They looked quite realistic—if you didn't look too closely.

People also found "dragon skulls" and complete "dragon skeletons" in caves. It had been assumed that dragons lived in caves. When people found a strange and unknown bone in a cave, they said it was a dragon's bone.

Some of these "dragon skeletons" are still around. Scientists today are able to identify them. The skeletons belonged to large animals like mammoths and cave bears that once lived in Europe. These animals died out thousands of years ago.

A typical "dragon skull" case occurred in 1673. A German doctor named Hayn was exploring caves in Central Europe. He found several strange-looking skulls. He thought they were dragon skulls. He even wrote an article on the subject of dragon skulls.

From Dr. Hayn's descriptions, scientists now know what kind of skulls he really found. They belonged to cave bears. These bears were much larger than any living bears. No one had ever seen a cave bear. In 1673, no one had any idea that there had ever been such an animal. But everyone had heard of dragons, although no one had ever seen a living dragon either. Still, it was easy to see how people thought the skulls belonged to dragons.

There is a dragon, of sorts, alive today. It is called the Komodo dragon. It is really the world's largest lizard. It can grow to a length of 12 feet and is very ferocious. The Komodo dragon lives in only one place, a small rugged island in the Pacific Ocean. The Komodo dragon was unknown to science until 1912. But it is possible that stories about it reached Europe much earlier. Exaggerated descriptions of this real animal might have become part of the dragon legend.

There is also a flying lizard, of sorts. Its scientific name is *Draco volans*. It is called the "flying dragon." It doesn't really fly—it glides. It has long

Two types of winged dragons

ribs, with skin stretched between them. This serves as the animal's "wings." The flying dragon lives in trees and can glide for about fifteen feet from tree limb to tree limb. But it isn't much of a dragon in size. It is only a few inches long when full-grown. It comes from the Malay islands in the Pacific Ocean, and is quite rare. But it is possible that stories about *Draco volans* reached Europe hundreds of years ago. These have been added to the dragon legend.

There is a more sensational possibility. Did the dragon legend originate with the dinosaurs? No creatures that ever lived looked more like dragons than dinosaurs. Like the dragons, dinosaurs were huge reptiles. Dinosaurs themselves didn't fly, but at the time of the dinosaurs, there were a number of large flying reptiles. These reptiles really flew too. They didn't just glide, like *Draco volans*. One of these flying reptiles had a wing span of 51 feet.

It sounds as though the dragon legend could have begun with the dinosaurs. Through the ages, stories about dinosaurs would have been confused and exaggerated. They might have been mixed up with the stories of flying lizards or the giant snakes.

But there is a problem with this theory. The problem is time. As far as we know, all the dinosaurs died out over 70 million years ago. That long ago, there were no people on the earth. So who could remember the dinosaurs? When scientists first discovered dinosaur bones, they were shocked. No one suspected that such monster-sized creatures had ever lived. Some early discoverers of dinosaur bones called them "dragon bones." But scientists today no longer identify dinosaurs with dragons.

Is it possible that some dinosaurs survived, so that people would know about them? They wouldn't have to be alive today. If they were alive even a few thousand years ago, they could have been seen by human beings.

There are some old stories about creatures that might have been dinosaurs. Even in recent years, there have been tales of people seeing dinosaurs on remote islands or dense jungles. But there has

Early-day drawings of dinosaurs made them
look like dragons.

never been any evidence to back up these stories.

Perhaps, someday, someone will find a very recent dinosaur bone or tooth. Perhaps even a living dinosaur will turn up. We should not say that anything is impossible. If that happens, we will have to reconsider the problem of dragons and dinosaurs. But until it does, we have to assume that dinosaurs died out long before anyone could remember them. For that reason we must assume that dinosaurs have nothing to do with dragons.

All that leaves us with only one real dragon. It is the original one—*draco,* the giant snake. The other dragon things—wings, legs, and the rest— were added on. People have a habit of making stories more fantastic and wonderful than they really are.

But that only explains the European dragon. Where did the good Chinese dragon come from?

The Chinese were more likely to have heard of the Komodo dragon. In fact, they probably did hear of it. Perhaps that was the model for their dragon. But there is a better one. It is the Chinese alligator.

The Chinese alligator is quite rare now, but a few hundred years ago it was found in rivers throughout China. It is the largest reptile in China —big enough and powerful enough to inspire the dragon legends.

In China, dragons are often associated with water. People thought that dragons controlled the tides and waves. Dragons were supposed to make the rain fall. And dragons lived in lakes and rivers. It is reasonable to assume that the creature that became the Chinese dragon was a water animal, a water animal like the alligator.

The Chinese never used the word "dragon." They called the creature the *lung*. When Westerners came to China, they saw pictures of the *lung*. It looked like the dragon, and so that is what they called it. But the dragon and the *lung* appear to have had different beginnings.

The Chinese made the same mistake about dragon bones that the Europeans did. Whenever the Chinese found the bones of unknown animals, they would call them "dragon bones." These "dragon bones" were very valuable in China. The Chinese ground the "dragon bones" to a fine powder. Then they took the powder as a cure for all sorts of diseases.

Less than fifty years ago, "dragon bones" were still being sold in Chinese drug stores. They were really the fossil teeth and bones of extinct animals. When a Western scientist went to China, he would go to the drug store, and look at the cabinets of "dragon bones." Many valuable fossils were found this way.

So, while there may never have been a fire-breathing dragon, the dragon stories were not completely made up either. Real animals inspired the dragon legends.

INDEX

Index